Contents

Meet the animals 4

Size and strength 6

Speed..8

Defence..10

Survival skills..12

Super senses..14

Deadly weapons 16

Fighting skills..18

Who wins?..20

Picture glossary 22

Find out more..23

Index..24

Meet the animals

What has **pincers** and a sharp tail?

It's the Emperor scorpion.

What has eight legs and a hairy body?

It's the
Goliath tarantula.

Would a scorpion or a tarantula win in a fight?
Let's find out!

Size and strength

If an Emperor scorpion sat on your arm, it would reach from your hand to your elbow. A scorpion's front legs are big to help it catch prey.

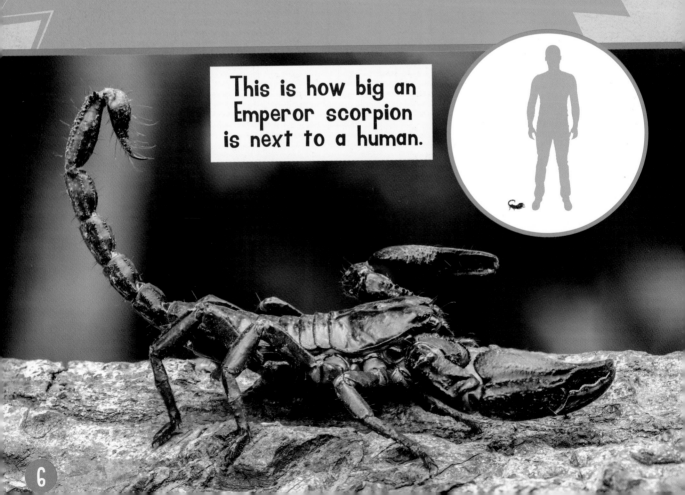

This is how big an Emperor scorpion is next to a human.

This is how big a
Goliath tarantula is
next to a human.

Even an Emperor scorpion is small
next to a Goliath tarantula! A Goliath
tarantula is big enough to drag a baby
bird out of its nest.

Speed

A scorpion **scuttles** quickly when it's striking at prey or trying to escape danger. A scorpion's front legs can crush an insect easily and give bigger animals a nasty nip.

A tarantula usually moves very slowly.
But it bursts into a run when chasing prey.
A tarantula doesn't need to spin webs.
It uses its strength to pounce on prey.

Defence

If there is nowhere to hide, a scorpion will stay as still as possible. Some fall into a deep sleep, as if they have been frightened to death.

A tarantula has hard skin. To let its body grow, a tarantula wriggles out of its old skin. Its body is soft and weak afterwards until the new skin hardens.

Survival skills

A scorpion is an incredible survivor. It can live without eating for a year. It can even be frozen in ice and walk away unhurt afterwards!

A tarantula likes to catch one meal every week in summer. Food is harder to catch in winter, so many tarantulas sleep through the winter in **burrows**.

Super senses

A scorpion has bad eyesight. Instead, its legs and **pincers** are covered in many small hairs. A scorpion uses these to sense movement.

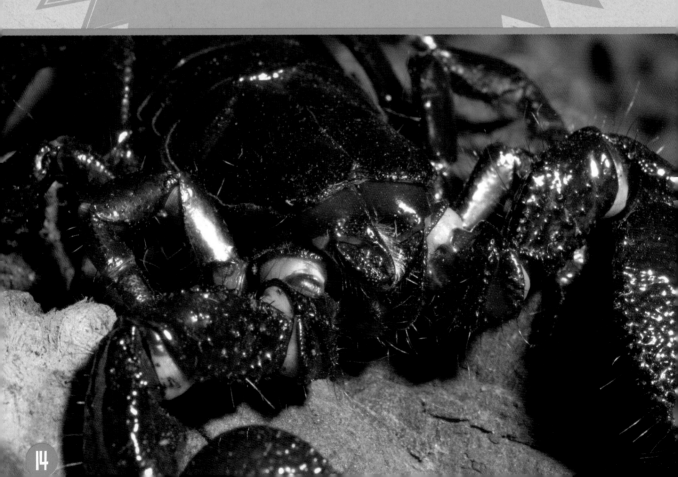

A tarantula's body is coloured to blend in. This lets it hide from enemies. A tarantula the colour of tree bark can sit on a tree without being spotted by hungry birds.

Deadly weapons

A scorpion's **sting** contains some of the strongest **venom** in the world. A scorpion grips prey in its large **pincers** while it jabs its sting into the **victim's** body.

sting

fang

A tarantula has two huge fangs. These are strong enough to bite through human skin. Before an insect can attack with a sting or pincers, a tarantula tries to bite it.

Fighting skills

With its **pincers** up and its **sting** pointed at the enemy, a scorpion will look terrifying. The **venom** in its tail can either kill an enemy or freeze it in its tracks.

A tarantula lifts its front legs up and shows
its fangs to warn it is about to attack. It
rubs its hairy legs together. This makes a
loud hissing noise to frighten the enemy.

Who wins?

What would happen if a scorpion faced a tarantula?

The tarantula would raise its front legs and hiss. The scorpion would flash its giant **pincers**.

But who would win?

	Scorpion	Tarantula
Size	7	10
Strength	8	6
Speed	7	7
Energy	10	9
Skin	9	9
Senses	8	8
Venom	10	7
Weapons	10	6
Fighting skills	8	10
Attack	10	8
TOTAL	**87/100**	80/100

SCORPION WINS!

Picture glossary

burrow animal's hole in the ground

pincer claw that can grip tightly

scuttle move along with lots of short, fast steps

sting part of an animal that can prick the skin and cause pain

venom toxic liquid passed into a victim's body through a bite or sting

victim someone who is harmed by a bad event

Find out more

Books

Deserts (What Animals Live Here?), M J Knight
(Franklin Watts, 2016)

Scorpions (Meet Desert Animals), Rose Davin
(Raintree, 2017)

Tarantula vs. Scorpion (Who Would Win?),
Jerry Pallotta (Scholastic, 2016)

Websites

kids.sandiegozoo.org/animals/insects/tarantula
Look at a fact file on tarantulas from San Diego Zoo
in the United States.

www.kidzone.ws/lw/spiders/facts-tarantula.htm
Find out more about the enemies of tarantulas.

**www.sciencekids.co.nz/sciencefacts/animals/
scorpion.html**
Read these fun facts about scorpions.

Index

burrows 13

colouring 15

covering 11, 14, 15

eyes 14

fangs 17

hairs 5, 14, 19

ice 12

legs 5, 8, 14, 20

liquid 19

pincers 4, 14, 16, 17, 18, 20

poison 16, 18, 19

sleep 10, 13

sting 16, 17, 18

summer 13

webs 9

winter 13